The search for
a better lawn
starts here!

Contents

Whether it's a tiny patch or a vast sward, the lawn is one element that few garden owners want to do without. It is, after all, such a versatile feature, providing a visual foil for flower and shrub borders as well as a great spot to relax and a safe place for children to play. But lawns can be troublesome: laying a new one is a daunting prospect, and even well-established lawns get plagued by weeds and moss. This book shows you how to achieve a great-looking lawn in a way that is safe for you and your family, pets and wildlife and how to keep it that way.

1

What makes a good lawn?

What **makes** a good lawn?

It depends what you want from your lawn! Everyone's an individual, every home is unique. Do you want a fine-ornamental lawn? A backdrop to a gorgeous flower border? A children's play ground? A hard wearing utility lawn, a wildlife grassy area or even a fragrant chamomile and herb lawn? The choice is always yours.

A good lawn is one which looks great throughout the year, doesn't require constant repair or attention and gives satisfaction to the owner, whether it's used to play on with children and pets or to entertain friends on a summer evening.

Why is a lawn so **important** to a garden?

For hundreds of years the British have been praised for the quality of their lawns. The English lawn is one of the reasons that our country has always been celebrated as a 'green and pleasant land'. In fact our style of lawn has been copied all over the world.

However, just as we take great care to decorate and furnish the rooms in our house, this exceptional room outside, requires planning and maintenance, both to ensure luxurious green growth and also to prevent weeds, pests and diseases taking over.

This book shows you:

- how to achieve a great looking lawn in a way that is safe for you, your family, pets and wildlife

- how to diagnose a sick lawn and make it better using only natural methods

- and how to keep it looking great

Renovate or replace?

If your lawn is very old and has not been cared for it will certainly be invaded by weeds, be uneven, washed-out and look tatty. It's easy to diagnose a worn-out lawn. Walk the lawn looking for yellow/light green colours, bare patches and weeds. If the lawn feels very springy then this is a sign of thatch (dead plant remains) which has built up and will encourage moss and disease. You can renovate a worn out lawn just by following the advice in this book in Chapter 4. However, if you want a truly outstanding lawn it may be best to start again.

Signs of a sick lawn
Dog bitch-scorch (top); dry, discoloured and patchy (middle); and (bottom) lawn invaded by weeds and moss.

Top 10 signs of a sick lawn

1 Discoloured pale green/yellow grass

2 Unevenly cut grass

3 Dead or dried-out grass

4 Uneven surfaces

5 Thatch causing a spongy surface

6 Hollows and bumps

7 Bare patches

8 Dog bitch-scorch (circles of yellow grass where your dog has urinated)

9 Invasion of weeds and moss

10 Turf diseases – like fairy rings and brown patch disease

To **seed** or to **turf?**

The big question any new lawn owner faces is whether to sow from seed or lay by turf. **Seeding may be cheaper but turf establishes more quickly and arguably provides a more uniform finish.** Turf quality is generally very good. Obviously you have to check that the turf contains the correct grass types for your needs and is from a reputable supplier. Also inspect the turves on delivery for weeds. Invariably chemical fertilizers and weed killers will have been used in growing the turf but they do not linger in the soil and should not affect your garden in the longer term. If in doubt ask the supplier exactly how the turf is treated.

Seeding is a cheaper option. A good tip is to order your seed mixture early in the year so that you get good quality seed and can sow when the conditions are right. If you leave it too late you might find that there is a shortage especially if the weather has been poor and yields are low. Typical sowing rates are 35-70g/m^2 which must be evenly spread over the surface – so measure your lawn area carefully before ordering. Always order a bit more than required then you can use the same type of seed for running repairs. If you want an alternative lawn such as chamomile, then you must grow from seed since turf is not available.

Choose the **lawn that is right** for you

There are thousands of different grasses to choose from but only a few that can withstand the regular cutting needed to produce a lush dense green lawn. Most often we blend rye, fescue and what are known as 'bent' grasses together to form the ideal home lawn.

The **ornamental lawn**, comes from fine leaved grasses such as bents and fescues growing in a needle-punch carpet style. With a gorgeous light green and soft texture many people like the luxurious elegance one of these lawns adds to their home. Beautiful to look at they may be, but they don't like heavy use. But if you have a sandy soil, this lawn will grow well provided you water regularly throughout the summer.

The **utility lawn** is perfect to take the rough and tumble of a growing family and pets. These are made from mixtures containing hard-wearing rye

From springy moss and weed filled patch to a level green sward – assess your lawn and then renovate, or replace.

grass and fescues. Rye grass has a thicker leaf blade and is much faster growing so damage is more quickly repaired. If you have a heavier soil including clay, these grasses will produce a rich dark green carpet that looks great all year round and is able to cope with hot dry summers when you forget to do the watering.

Chamomile or herb lawns don't require much mowing and might be an attractive option for a small sunny area of lawn. Alternatively, if you have made room for a **wildlife area** in the garden, you might think about a **wildflower lawn**. Here you can tolerate some of those weeds. Relax your mowing regime, cutting just a few times a year. Traditional hay meadows are cut just once (in August), but flowers are best encouraged by cutting in June and September, with a hand-shear trim occasionally if it gets too untidy. Don't add any fertiliser, contrary to other gardening practice, wildflowers actually do best in soils with low nutrients. Clear away the cuttings to the compost heap. As well as looking pretty, punctuated by flowers, the longer grass offers shelter to insects and other small creatures.

The **natural** approach

Why **avoid** chemicals?

The modern approach to getting good quality lawns has been to use chemical aids. This might be as a seed dressing, fertilizer coating or control for pests and diseases. In most cases this involves using man-made synthetic chemicals. The long-term effect of these chemicals on our environment is unclear. Certainly chemical residues are appearing in water supplies and the food chain and these seem to be affecting the ecology of our environment. Of course dosing your lawn regularly with chemicals can also be an expensive business.

We believe a better approach is to work with nature to produce a vibrant lawn. It is possible to create and maintain a beautiful lawn by using **sound management principles** and only those **organic naturally occurring chemicals** that biodegrade harmlessly back into the environment. With the help of modern tools it need not even be hard work!

In this book we show you how to achieve a great lawn through regular mowing, composting, raking, scarification, aeration, spiking, top dressing, manual weeding and working with worms. And don't worry, if you're not familiar with these terms they will be explained as we go along.

action stations

1 **Choose** the right lawn for your home. Will it be ornamental, utility, wildlife or chamomile? Check if your soil is sandy or clay.

2 **Renovate or replace?** Depending upon the condition of your lawn decide whether to renovate the existing lawn or replace with new.

3 **Decide** on turf or seed. As a rule of thumb, turf is quicker but seed is cheaper.

4 **Order** turf and seed early in the year. Avoid problems from late supplies.

2

Know your lawn

Know **your lawn**

Grass is an excellent plant for gardens. It grows from the base of the plant near the soil, all year round even at low temperatures. This is why it always regrows after cutting.

Through understanding nature's natural cycles of growth we can manage the lawn to always be in the best condition.

Lawn grasses work in harmony with the soil and atmosphere to produce lush growth. Grass spreads by horizontally spreading stems called rhizomes (underground) and stolons (overground). This is called tillering. We can manage the lawn to encourage this growth and ensure an increasingly dense carpet of leaf blades. Grass is a very shallow fibrous rooting plant and easily suffers from drought in hot weather.

From the soil, grass takes nutrients including nitrogen (N) for growing, phosphorus (P) for roots, potassium (K) for disease resistance and cell strength and magnesium (Mg) to help turn sunlight into sugar (photosynthesis). However, just three N, P and K are needed as fertilizers. Plenty of air is needed in the soil to encourage growth and prevent disease. That's why we need to aerate the soil regularly and keep off the lawn in wet weather to avoid compaction.

Mowing

How you cut your lawn will have a major impact on how it looks. Mowing will help to weaken and kill off-weeds. However, the more vigorous weeds may take 2-3 years to die until all the stored energy in their roots has been exhausted from the constant pressure of mowing.

Cutting too short too often will also weaken the grass. First decide on how short you want your grass. Then set your mower blades to the right height to maintain the appearance you want.

On an ornamental lawn this could be 0.5-1.0cm and on a utility lawn 2.5-5cm tall. The finer the grass the closer the mow. Mowing should take place regularly and the grass should not be allowed to grow more than twice the desired height before cutting. But beware of consistently cutting your lawn too short – you might scalp the turf and encourage weeds.

Before mowing it's a good idea to brush debris away and work worm casts into the soil. Brushing also raises the grass up to meet the mower blade. While you're doing this make a mental note of any unevenness or weeds which you will have to deal with later.

The next question is **which lawn mower?** You have two choices either a **rotary or cylinder** mower. If you want neat stripes down the turf you simply have to have a

Cylinder or rotary mower? Cylinder for stripes and ornamental lawns, rotary for utility lawns and speed.

Always collect your clippings. Leaving them on the lawn will add mulch and encourage moss. Place them on your compost where they will add nitrogen and potassium.

cylinder mower and cut each strip in opposite directions. Cylinders cut with a scissors type action and also remove clippings better. They produce a fine even cut suited to ornamental lawns. Mow them every 2-3 days down to 5-12mm in the summer. Increase the height of cut in the autumn and winter to 15-20mm.

If you have a utility or chamomile lawn and are not bothered about stripes, then a rotary mower will give excellent results. They are also ideal for cutting down long or rough grass and for use on uneven surfaces. The height of cut is generally higher at 10-25mm rising to 30-40mm over winter.

Every time you cut, change the direction of mowing to help kill weeds and cover the whole lawn.

Although grass is about 95% water, after a few weeks on the compost heap it will shrink to less than a quarter of its original volume. However, it decomposes slowly; add some leaves or other woody material to help speed up the process.

Clippings

Lawns produce huge amounts of grass clippings. Because of this some people leave them on the lawn after mowing rather than disposing of them properly. This is wrong because it builds up spongy dead plant remains called 'thatch' and encourages moss. This then has to be removed by a hard rake (scarification). Most lawn mowers have a collection box where the cut clippings are stored. This is called 'boxed-off' and it is essential that all clippings are 'boxed-off' at every mowing.

Clippings are rich in nitrogen and potassium. The best solution is to pile them into a compost heap at the bottom of the garden and let nature decompose them. The next season the composted clippings can be spread onto the flower beds where they increase the water reserve of the soil, smother out any weeds and supply some extra nutrients.

Weeds

A weed is simply any plant growing in the wrong place. Typical weeds of turf include; annual Meadow grass *Poa annual*, dandelion *Taraxacum officinale,* daisies *Bellis perennis*, plantains *Plantago* sp, buttercup *Ranunculus repens,* white clover *Trifolium repens*, Yarrow *Achillea millifolium* and moss.

Weeds are easy to spot. Walk the lawn and if you see something that isn't grass then it's a weed and needs to be removed. The low growing weeds survive because they are untouched by the mower. They are easily spotted by their rosette patterned leaves hugging the soil.

For the most part weeds are kept under control by regular mowing, aeration and scarification. If you leave it too long between cuts other weeds such as groundsel *Senecio vulgaris*, couch grass *Agropyron repens* and thistles *Cirsium arvense* may also invade. Even a quick rake before mowing will help to keep weeds at bay.

Weeding: A good way for your children to earn some pocket money! Extract weeds with a small trowel or knife ensuring that all of the root is removed.

The most environmentally friendly way to remove weeds is to dig them up with a small trowel or knife making certain that all the root is removed.

Some weeds, like clover are beneficial in lawns as they fix nitrogen from the atmosphere and can stimulate healthy green grass growth. However, clover left completely unchecked can take over. Altering the height of mower cut will enable you to acheive the desired grass/clover balance on a utility lawn. For an ornamental lawn you should apply a more strict mowing and raking regime.

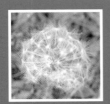   

Weeds (from top left): Dandelion seed, dandelion in flower, clover, annual meadow grass, buttercup and yarrow. Depending upon the kind of lawn you want, you can banish weeds completely or, if you prefer, tolerate a little diversity.

Working with **worms**

At first glance earthworms are a nuisance to us because of the unsightly worm casts left on the surface. However, in reality they are useful because they create aeration and drainage channels in the soil helping to maintain a healthy lawn.

Earthworms also help to:

- reduce fertilizer use because casts are rich in nutrients
- mix dead and decaying plant remains
- rotavate the soil
- stimulate root growth
- increase availability of plant nutrients
- assist with nutrient recycling
- supply food for some ground feeding birds such as blackbird, robin and thrush

That's why we welcome worms in the lawn. The casts can easily be brushed in leaving a beautiful lawn behind. If you find any worms on the surface pick them up and put them straight onto the compost heap where they will love munching through old plant remains.

action stations

① **Choose your mower** – Cylinder for stripes or rotary for speed.

② **Clippings** – prepare an area of garden to use as a compost heap to dump 'boxed off' clippings.

③ **Weeds** – dig up and remove using a trowel or knife.

3

Creating your perfect lawn

Creating your perfect lawn

Everyone wants a perfect lawn. But the key to success is preparation. Get all the tools and equipment you need together before you start and take the time to prepare a flat surface on which to lay turf or sow seed.

Prepare the **soil**

1   Remove and dispose of all the existing turf or plant material onto the compost heap.

2   Go over the soil and remove all the unwanted large stones, bits of wood or other material that will hinder a perfectly flat surface.

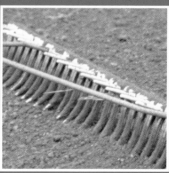

Preparation, preparation, preparation – the key to success. Top: Cleared and rotavated. Above: Hard raking to create a level surface.

3   If your soil is very compacted this is also the time to rotavate or dig it over to create a well drained and aerated lawn.

4   Rake the soil hard into a level surface. Break up the large lumps as you go. If your soil is very uneven you will need to buy some top soil to spread into the hollows and then rake. Keep raking level. After a while your eye will be fine-tuned to the ground and you will easily see any hollows that need filling or peaks that need levelling. If you prefer, you can use a long spirit level to check your accuracy.

5   Walk the soil firming it with your heel so that the lawn won't sink when you walk on it. When you're satisfied with the surface you are ready to sow seed or lay turf.

Adding top soil to an uneven and troublesome surface (top). Walking the soil (above) to prevent your lawn from sinking.

Turf laying

The best time to lay turf is autumn or early spring allowing the roots to grow firmly into the soil. The golden rule of laying turf is 'never walk on it'. Everything you do must prevent this by using boards to spread your weight. Make certain you use a reputable supplier for a quality turf. Don't buy meadow grass from the local farm! It will be peppered with weeds.

1   Just before you start laying, rake the patch where the turf is going down again to ensure it is level.

2   Unroll the turf and start laying it along one edge, working backwards from this point. You can move the turf around on the soil using a fork and make sure that the edges butt-up together tightly. When you lay the next row start in a different place so that all the joins are not in the same place – as you would if you were laying a wood floor.

3   Use a sharp knife or half-moon iron to cut the edges or trim the turf to the shape you want. To get an immediate striped effect simply lay each row in opposite directions. When your lawn is well rooted the stripes can be maintained by mowing each strip in opposite directions.

4 Firm the newly laid turf so that the roots are in close contact with the soil. To do this lay out walking boards and walk over the entire lawn, moving the boards around to make certain that every inch of turf is covered.

5 Use a hose with a fine rose and thoroughly water the new turf so that it gets off to a good start. If the weather is hot you will have to keep watering every few days until the grass is established. This will take 2-3 weeks.

6 Give the turf a good chance to get established. Keep off the grass (for at least 10 days) until you are certain it has properly rooted into the soil and won't move when you step on it.

To get an immediate striped effect, lay your rows of turf in opposite directions. Walk the plank to ensure that newly laid turf is firmed and that the roots are in contact with the soil.

Pour yourself a cool drink, grab a chair and then sit back and enjoy.

Seed sowing

Sowing seed is easy and many people prefer it to turf laying. But care is needed to ensure even sowing. Seeding is also used to repair bare patches. The best times of year to sow are spring and early autumn, although grass will germinate throughout the year, especially if the weather is mild. After 10 days the seeds will have germinated and the leaf blades will be showing.

1   Mark out the soil into $1m^2$ blocks and sprinkle the seed into each square. If you have a large garden to sow, hire a seed drill calibrated for grass. It will save time and give you a very even finish.

Seed sowing aftercare: Water regularly and first mow when grass is 8cm high.

2   Most grasses are sown at about 35g/m², but check the packet and follow the supplier's instructions. Sowing is completed in two passes. Half is sown in one direction then the second half at right angles to the first. Another technique is to mix the seed with some topsoil or sand which is then raked evenly over the whole lawn area.

3   Either use a roller on the seed bed or walk over it on boards to firm the seed into the soil.

4   Water the seed bed with a fine spray to encourage germination. Keep watering every few days so that it doesn't dry out.

5   Stop birds eating your seed and dust-bathing. Try tightly stretched black netting or string tied with lengths of silver foil, raised above the bed. This usually deters birds quite well.

After **care**

1   Water regularly making sure that the seed or turf does not dry out. Do not walk on the new surface until you are sure it has properly rooted.

2   First mow when grass is 8cm high gradually reducing the height of the cut down to 1cm over the season.

action stations

① **Preparation:** Spend time clearing, digging and rotavating the surface. Rake over the soil until it's totally flat; add topsoil to troublesome uneven surfaces.

② **Lay turf in rows** going in opposite directions to achieve an immediate striped effect. Use boards to walk on it. Use a sharp knife or edging iron to cut the edges.

③ **Sowing:** Sow evenly at about 35g/m^2. Use netting or string to stop birds eating your seed.

④ **Aftercare** (turf): Keep off the grass for at least 10 days or until you're certain it has established properly.
Mowing (seeded lawn): First mow when grass is 8cm high.
Water lawns thoroughly, especially in hot weather.

Improving and maintaining

Methods and tools for improving and maintaining an existing lawn

As your lawn gets older the biggest problem will be weeds invading the sward. Get into the habit now of inspecting your lawn for colour, weeds, thatch, moss and worn out patches that might need replacing or overseeding. We will show you how to improve and maintain a first rate lawn through good lawnsmanship.

Aeration

A major part of good lawn management is to get air into the soil so that the roots can flourish and also to create drainage channels to remove excess water. Lawns suffer from heavy pedestrian traffic causing compaction. Aeration helps to correct this and maintain your lawn in top condition.

Forking. The simplest form of aeration. Just walk over the lawn stabbing the ground with your garden fork. Make sure it goes in at least 100 mm. Keep walking as you do this creating some heave as you bend the fork in the soil.

Solid-tining

These produce a more even pattern of aeration channels. It's very easy to do. Just keep rolling the wheeled aerator all over the lawn. These machines are also excellent at breaking up a thatch layer.

Hollow-tining

More complex aeration technique. A core of soil is removed creating a much larger and more stable channel. This makes it ideal for lawns on clay or waterlogged soils. Waste soil cores are swept up afterwards and deposited on the compost heap.

Aeration, solid-tining and hollow-tining: Forking is the simplest form of aeration; solid-tining produces an even pattern of aeration channels whilst hollow-tining removes a core of soil and is ideal on waterlogged soils.

Top dressing

After aeration treatments it's a good idea to apply a 1:3:6 ratio peat-substitute/soil/sand top-dressing to fill hollows and encourage dense grass growth. These are easily bought from the garden centre or you can use John Innes soil-based potting compost. These should be spread on the soil and raked in evenly. This helps to maintain an even surface and also fills the cavities caused by frost, roots and worms creating excellent drainage and aeration channels. It is especially important for the fine grasses of an ornamental lawn. After you've finished raking and brushing no top dressing should be left visible on the grass surface.

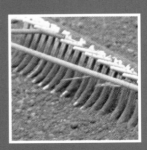

After aeration and scarifying, apply a top dressing to fill hollows and encourage growth.

Fertilizer

New lawns look great for the first season. After that they will need regular fertilizer to keep them looking green, lush and disease free. **Organic fertilizers** suitable for lawns are made from recycled animal materials. Don't forget to read and follow the manufacturer's instructions. Because these fertilizers are organic, nutrient contents may vary from the guide given below.

Nitrogen (N)

Why: To produce dark green leaves. **When:** Spring and summer.

What: Hoof and horn (13% N, 14% P). A slow release source of nitrogen and phosphorus,suitable for lawns where some extra green colour is needed.

(If you are a little squeamish when it comes to handling fertilizers remember that most products have been heat-sterilized prior to sale. If you are in any doubt, or have any other concerns, check with the manufacturer – and remember, always wear gloves when handling any fertilizer and ensure that any cuts are properly covered).

How: Apply 30-60 g/m2 in spring; 40-60 g/m2 in summer reducing to 7-20g/m2 in the autumn

Phosphorus (P)

Why: To increase root growth. **When:** Autumn

What: Sterilized bone meal (22%P). A very safe slow release fertilizer to encourage strong root growth. Phosphorus is very difficult to supply as a fertilizer. The nutrient when in solution in the soil quickly forms chemical bonds and becomes unavailable to plant roots. Organic sources are very useful since the fertilizer is broken down slowly by bacteria and micro-organisms to gradually release phosphorus into the soil.

How: Apply 27-55g/m2 in the autumn.

Potassium (K)

Why: To build disease resistance. **When:** Spring and autumn.

What: Ground rock potash (50% K). Mined rock potash crushed and treated Potassium is abundant in the natural world and these fertilizers are safe for your health and to use in the environment.

How: Apply 8-16 g/m2 in spring and again in the autumn

Compound fertilizers

There are also some compound organic fertilizers like '6x Organic fertilizer' (5%N, 3.3% P, 2.2% K) which you might prefer to use as a general purpose fertilizer. Another good one is 'Organic spike and spread' from www.perfect-blend.co.uk which is purpose made for turf. Use these according to the manufacturer's instructions.

Through the **seasons**

Winter

Even in winter there is work to do. Remember that in frost, snow or very wet weather leave the turf well alone or you will cause damage to the grass and compact the soil.

The key activity is to aerate the soil, both to allow water to escape from the surface and also to enable air to circulate and stimulate root growth in the spring. You can either hire a machine or walk the lawn spiking with a garden fork.

Keep weeding and scarifying (hard raking) regularly throughout the winter until you are certain that all the thatch (dead plant remains) has been removed.

Spring

Your lawn should be disease-free and healthy following the winter maintenance schedule. In spring the grass is ready to explode into new growth. Start mowing regularly. Tidy up lawn edges. Make sure that you use a nitrogen and potassium fertilizer. Dig up and remove any weeds. Re-seed bare batches and lay any new turf. Now is the best time to sow chamomile seeds too.

Summer

The lawn will be growing vigorously. Keep cutting the grass at the correct height for your use. This could be as low as 0.5-1.0cm on an ornamental lawn to 5.0cm on a utility lawn used by children and pets. In drought conditions raise the height of cut. Mowing is easily the most important task

Sharpen your mower blades annually and regularly remove built up debris.

to affect the quality of your lawn. Box-off and remove all the clippings to the compost heap or they will cause thatch and encourage both moss and disease. Scarify to remove moss and weeds. Chamomile lawns only need a light trim with shears to keep them neat and tidy. Use a nitrogen fertilizer to encourage leaf growth. Keep weeding. If it is very hot you will also need to water the lawn every few days.

Autumn is the time to scarify (hard rake) the lawn to reduce moss and remove dead and decaying plant material.

Autumn

Keep cutting the lawn to remove the new growth. Grass can keep growing at low temperatures so try to get the last cut in before winter. The focus in autumn is on disease resistance as the wet weather starts, and establishing an extended root system to support the lawn next spring. This is achieved by a fertilizer containing just phosphorus and potassium.

Autumn is also the time to scarify (hard rake) the lawn to remove all the dead and decaying plant material that would cause thatch and encourage diseases. Keep weeding by hand to remove any undesirable plants.
Sow any bare patches and lay new turf. Raise the height of cut as winter approaches. Complete your aeration programme. Repair bumps and hollows with top soil. If the hollow is more than 2.5cm deep then cut the turf open and insert new top soil under the turf making sure that it is level.

Top tips for
perfect lawns

- **Choose** a lawn that is right for you – ornamental, utility, wildlife or even a chamomile or herb
- **Preparation** of the soil is the key to success. Rake soil into an even surface
- Use **high quality** turf or seed
- **Brush** your lawn before mowing
- **Mow** regularly. Keep the grass short and weeds under control
- **Remove** clippings – use a box on your mower. Leave nothing behind to cause thatch and disease
- **Scarify** in spring and autumn to remove old grass and weeds
- **Aerate** the soil using a fork or tiner
- **Walk** the lawn removing all weeds using a trowel or knife
- **Water** regularly in hot weather
- **Trim** the edges for a perfect finish
- **Buy** just enough organic fertilizers to use each year

Owning and managing a lawn is something everyone can enjoy. It is a rewarding experience to see how your work pays off. If you follow the advice given in this book you should get an attractive lawn and hours of enjoyment for yourself and your family. Look forward to those hot summer days stretched out on the lawn in your chair or enjoying a family barbecue.

– Good luck and happy lawnsmanship!

Resources

Useful websites

www.perfect-blend.co.uk – A leading manufacturer of organic plant foods

www.gonegardening.com – On-line gardening store

www.organicseeds.co.uk – selection of turf and chamomile seed

www.organic-concentrates.co.uk – Supplier of 6X-organic fertilizer

www.rolawn.co.uk – The leading supplier of high quality turf in the UK

www.garden-lawn-seed.co.uk – Specialist lawn seeds

www.britishseedhouses.com – National suppliers network

www.doctorgreenfingers.co.uk – General gardening help and advice clinic

Books

L. V. Brown 2002 *"Applied principles of Horticultural Science" 2nd Edition*
Butterworth-Heinemann

▍Acknowledgements

The author (Laurie Brown) wishes to acknowledge the assistance given by:

Rolawn Turf Growers Ltd

Rob Ayres, Raycox Turf Ltd

Ian Clarke, Liberty Landscapes

Lee Driver, Berkshire College of Agriculture

My brother Richard Brown and nieces & nephew Philippa, Nicola, Rebecca and Ben, all of whom helped with the photography.